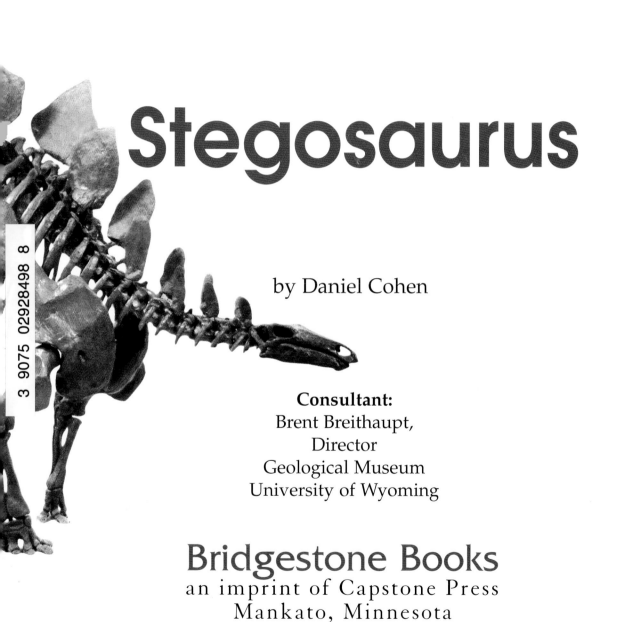

Stegosaurus

by Daniel Cohen

Consultant:
Brent Breithaupt,
Director
Geological Museum
University of Wyoming

Bridgestone Books
an imprint of Capstone Press
Mankato, Minnesota

Bridgestone Books are published by Capstone Press
151 Good Counsel Drive, P.O. Box 669, Mankato, Minnesota 56002
http://www.capstone-press.com

Library of Congress Cataloging-in-Publication Data
Cohen, Daniel, 1936–
    Stegosaurus/by Daniel Cohen.
    p. cm.—(The Bridgestone Science Library)
    Includes bibliographical references and index.
    Summary: Discusses the physical characteristics, food, habitat, relatives, and
extinction of the slow-moving vegetarian dinosaur, Stegosaurus.
    ISBN 0-7368-0618-0
    1. Stegosaurus—Juvenile literature. [1. Stegosaurus. 2. The Bridgestone Science
Library.] I. Title. II. Series.
QE862.O65 C625 2001
567.915′3—dc21   00-021737

Editorial Credits
Erika Mikkelson, editor; Linda Clavel, cover designer and illustrator; Heidi Schoof
    and Kimberly Danger, photo researchers

Photo Credits
American Museum of Natural History, 10–11
David F. Clobes, 20
Francois Gohier, 16
The Natural History Museum/Orbis, 8
Unicorn Stock Photos/Richard Dippold, 14
Visuals Unlimited/A. J. Copley, cover, 1; Ken Lucas, 4–5, 6, 12

1 2 3 4 5 6 06 05 04 03 02 01

Table of Contents

Stegosaurus compared to a 5-foot-tall
(1.5-meter-tall) human

Stegosaurus

The name Stegosaurus (STEG-oh-SORE-us) means roofed reptile. A staggered row of flat, bony plates ran down the dinosaur's neck, back, and tail. Stegosaurus was a large dinosaur. It measured 25 feet (7.5 meters) from nose to tail. It weighed about 2 tons (1.8 metric tons).

staggered
placed in an uneven pattern

5

The World of Stegosaurus

Stegosaurus lived about 150 million years ago. Earth looked different then. Earth's land masses were closer together. The weather was warm and wet. Giant ferns and other tropical plants covered the land.

tropical
anything related to warm and wet weather

This dinosaur is Kentrosaurus.
Kentrosaurus and Stegosaurus
were stegosaurids.

Relatives of Stegosaurus

Stegosaurus belonged to a group of
dinosaurs called stegosaurids.
Stegosaurids were dinosaurs with plates
or spikes on their bodies. Kentrosaurus
(KEN-troh-SORE-us) was a stegosaurid.
It had sharp spikes on its back and tail.
Its name means prickly reptile.

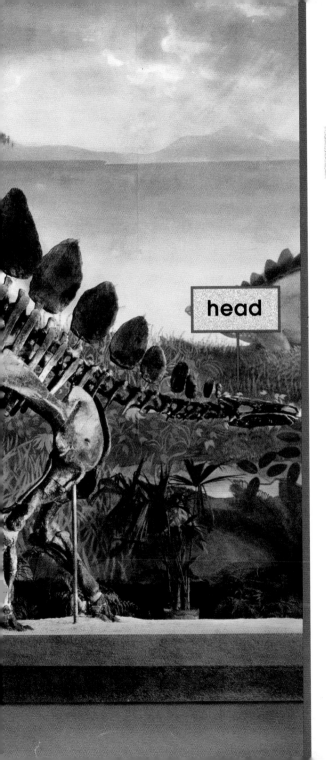

head

Parts of Stegosaurus

Stegosaurus had a tiny head, a thick body, and a powerful tail. The slow-moving Stegosaurus walked on four legs. The dinosaur used spikes at the end of its tail as a weapon. The staggered plates on Stegosaurus's back probably controlled its body temperature.

A Tiny Brain

Stegosaurus's brain was tiny compared to the size of its body. Stegosaurus's brain was one of the smallest of any dinosaur.

What Stegosaurus Ate

Stegosaurus was a plant eater. It could not lift its head very high off the ground. The dinosaur ate ferns and other plants that grew close to the ground. Stegosaurus may have traveled in groups for protection when it ate.

The End of Stegosaurus

Stegosaurus became extinct about 135 million years ago. Other stegosaurids and all other dinosaurs disappeared from Earth about 65 million years ago. Scientists are not sure why all the dinosaurs died.

extinct
no longer living anywhere in the world

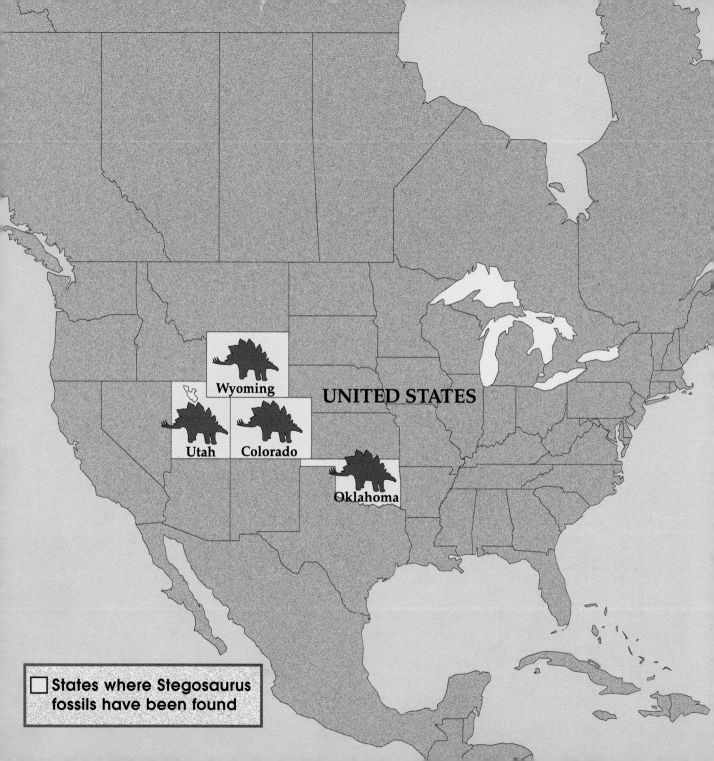

UNITED STATES

Wyoming

Utah   Colorado

Oklahoma

☐ States where Stegosaurus
fossils have been found

Discovering Stegosaurus

In 1876, M. P. Felch found the first Stegosaurus fossils in Colorado. Paleontologist Othniel Charles Marsh named the fossils Stegosaurus in 1877. In 1885, Felch also discovered a nearly complete Stegosaurus skeleton in Colorado.

paleontologist
a scientist who finds and studies fossils

Not In Kansas Anymore

Studying Stegosaurus Today

Paleontologists continue to study Stegosaurus fossils. In the past, some scientists believed the bony plates protected the dinosaur. Today, most paleontologists believe the plates helped control Stegosaurus's body temperature.

Hands On: Digging for Fossils

Paleontologists dig for dinosaur bones in rocks and dirt. Digging the bones out of rock or dirt without breaking them is difficult. You can see how difficult it is by doing this activity.

What You Need

A sheet of newspaper
A large chocolate chip cookie
Toothpicks
Tweezers
Small, soft paintbrush

What You Do

1. Set the cookie on a sheet of newspaper.
2. Use the toothpicks to dig the chocolate chips out of the cookie. The chocolate chips are like bones. The cookie is like a rock.
3. Hold a chocolate chip with the tweezers over the newspaper. Brush the cookie crumbs off with the paintbrush.
4. Try not to break or damage the chips.

Words to Know

dinosaur (DYE-na-sore)—an extinct land reptile; dinosaurs lived on Earth for more than 150 million years.

fossil (FOSS-uhl)—any remains or traces of past life; bones and footprints can be fossils.

paleontologist (PAY-lee-on-TOL-ah-jist)—a scientist who finds and studies fossils

reptile (REP-tile)—a cold-blooded animal with a backbone; scales cover a reptile's body.

Read More

Riehecky, Janet. *Stegosaurus: The Plated Dinosaur.* Dinosaur Days. New York: Benchmark Books, 1998.

Rodriguez, K. S. *Stegosaurus.* Prehistoric Creatures Then and Now. Austin, Texas: Steadwell Books, 2000.

Internet Sites

American Museum of Natural History: Stegosaurus
http://www.amnh.org/Exhibition/Expedition/Fossils/
Specimens/stegosaurus.html
Zoom Dinosaurs
http://www.EnchantedLearning.com/subjects/dinosaurs

Index